DEC   2015

Amazing Robots

Robots in Medicine

Richard and Louise Spilsbury

Gareth Stevens
PUBLISHING

Please visit our website, **www.garethstevens.com**.
For a free color catalog of all our high-quality books,
call toll free 1-800-542-2595 or fax 1-877-542-2596.

Library of Congress Cataloging-in-Publication Data
Spilsbury, Richard.
Robots in medicine / by Richard and Louise Spilsbury.
p. cm. — (Amazing robots)
Includes index.
ISBN 978-1-4824-3009-7 (pbk.)
ISBN 978-1-4824-3012-7 (6 pack)
ISBN 978-1-4824-3010-3 (library binding)
1. Robotics — Juvenile literature. 2. Robotics in medicine — Juvenile literature.
I. Spilsbury, Richard, 1963-. II. Spilsbury, Louise. III. Title.
TJ211.2 S65 2016
629.8—d23

First Edition

Published in 2016 by
Gareth Stevens Publishing
111 East 14th Street, Suite 349
New York, NY 10003

© 2016 Gareth Stevens Publishing

Produced for Gareth Stevens by Calcium
Editors for Calcium: Sarah Eason and Jennifer Sanderson
Designers: Paul Myerscough and Simon Borrough
Picture researcher: Susannah Jayes

Photo credits: Cover: DARPA: Courtesy of the Johns Hopkins University Applied Physics Laboratory;
Inside: ROBOT-Rx® image courtesy of Aesynt Incorporated 24-25; Argo Medical Technologies
GmbH: 38; DARPA: Courtesy of the Johns Hopkins University Applied Physics Laboratory 41;
Dreamstime: Lculig 22, Stratum 23; Courtesy of El Camino Hospital, California: 33; Given Imaging:
20; Intelligent Hospital Systems: 26, 27; Intouchhealth: 1, 30, 31; ©2014 Intuitive Surgical, Inc
12-13, 14, 15; Matia Robotics: 37; Panasonic: 32; RSLSteeper 42, 43; Second Sight Medical Products
44, 45; Shutterstock: Beloborod 7, catwalker 4, daseaford 35, EPSTOCK 18, Attila JANDI 5, khuruzero
40, Levent Konuk 19, Poznyakov 11, Valentina Razumova 17, Oliver Sved 16, Vshivkova 21t,
XiXinXing 6; US Navy: Mass Communication Specialist 1st Class Brien Aho 8; Wikimedia Commons:
Euchiasmus 21c, Steve Jurvetson 39, NASA 10, Nimur 9; Xenex: 29.

Printed in the United States of America
CPSIA compliance information: Batch #CS15GS: For further information contact Gareth Stevens, New York, New York at 1-800-542-2595.

Contents

chapter 1

Bot Doctors

If you have ever watched a movie or television program set in the future, the medical facilities are often staffed by robots. These robots perform surgery, give injections, and even fit false limbs. Robot doctors are not just the health care workers of the distant future—they are already working in medicine today.

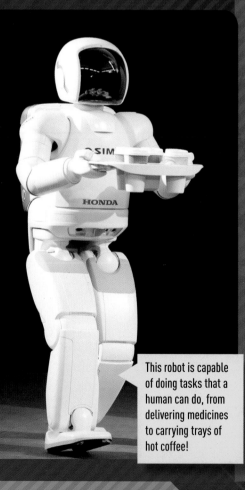

This robot is capable of doing tasks that a human can do, from delivering medicines to carrying trays of hot coffee!

What Are Medical Robots?

Robots are machines capable of performing actions automatically. Some are controlled by computers that are programmed by people. These programs command the robot to carry out a sequence of movements, using parts often operated by motors. The robots may be operated by remote control. Other robots are devices that are controlled directly by human movements. For example, some robot surgical equipment moves only when a real surgeon's hands move. The imaginary robots from movies often look rather like people—they are humanoid robots. However, many medical robots are not humanoid, but come in all shapes and sizes. Some are rooms with robotic arms that dispense drugs, while others are tiny capsules that patients swallow to take pictures of the inside of their body.

The Benefit of Robots

Medical work is specialized and requires lengthy training and great experience. However, some tasks are time-consuming and tedious, and humans can make mistakes. This is one way in which robots can make a difference. For example, robots can scan and analyze radiographs more quickly and cheaply than people, but in most cases, just as accurately. Using robots can free up time for health care staff to do other things that robots mostly cannot, such as reassuring sick patients or interpreting the most complicated radiographs. However, robots can also do things that people cannot. For example, a surgeon can sit in a hospital in one country and perform surgery in a hospital in another using robot technology.

In the future, humanoid doctors—robots that look, talk, and behave like a real doctor—may work alongside human doctors in hospitals.

Robots Are the Future

Today, medical robots are controlled or programmed in their actions by human operators. In the future, medical robots might be able to act independently and become truly smart. That means making decisions and movements themselves, using brain-like memory banks. Smart robot doctors might be able to make diagnoses of some illnesses. Abilities like these could change the face of medicine completely and make it possible for people worldwide, even in the poorest countries, to have better access to quality health care.

Minimal Surgery

Surgery can be uncomfortable and risky for patients. Patients are often given general anesthetic to keep them still and prevent them from feeling pain during operations, but anesthetic drugs can be harmful unless very carefully monitored. Large incisions through skin, bone, and layers of muscle to reach body parts inside, such as organs or joints, can cause tissue damage that takes a long time to heal. Bleeding caused by the cutting of blood vessels during open surgery can weaken patients. The longer an incision is open, the higher the risk of germs getting inside and causing infection. After surgery, patients usually need to stay in the hospital to recover. During this time they may require care to monitor and treat pain and infections during healing, and blood transfusions to replace lost blood. Patients may also be left with scars.

Through a Keyhole

During the late twentieth century, doctors developed a type of surgery that was less risky. The new surgery also had a lower impact on patients after their operations because it used small incisions. Small incisions mean smaller scars, less bleeding, and faster recovery after surgery so patients spend less time in the hospital. In laparoscopy, or keyhole surgery, surgeons often use local anesthetic to numb just the surgical area. They make a hole and poke in a tiny camera and light—called an endoscope—along with tiny surgical tools, like mini scissors, which they move by using long, straight rods.

In keyhole surgery, surgeons operate on what they can see through the camera by moving the tools.

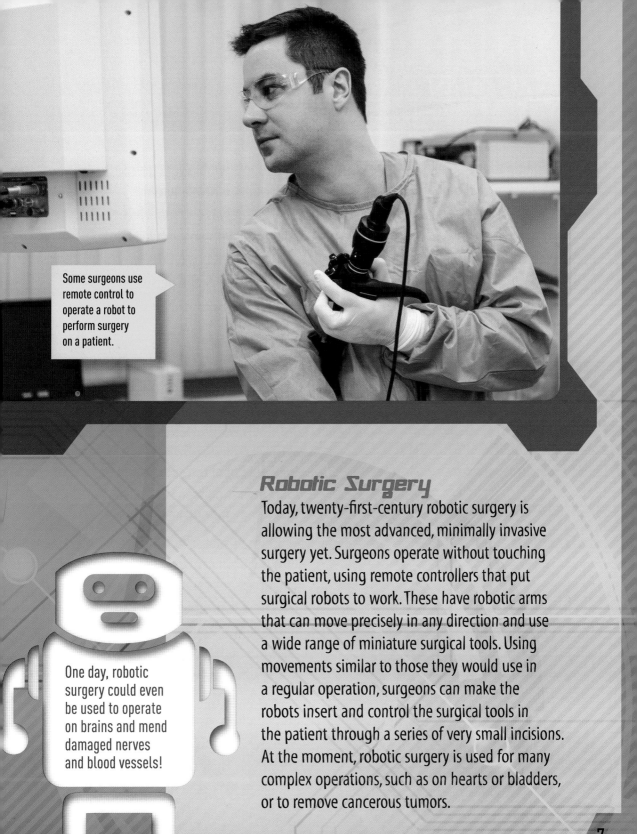

Some surgeons use remote control to operate a robot to perform surgery on a patient.

One day, robotic surgery could even be used to operate on brains and mend damaged nerves and blood vessels!

Robotic Surgery

Today, twenty-first-century robotic surgery is allowing the most advanced, minimally invasive surgery yet. Surgeons operate without touching the patient, using remote controllers that put surgical robots to work. These have robotic arms that can move precisely in any direction and use a wide range of miniature surgical tools. Using movements similar to those they would use in a regular operation, surgeons can make the robots insert and control the surgical tools in the patient through a series of very small incisions. At the moment, robotic surgery is used for many complex operations, such as on hearts or bladders, or to remove cancerous tumors.

Precise Work

In addition to their ability to work in small spaces, robots enable very precise work, time after time. This is critical for many procedures, where a wrong move could have serious impact. For example, laser surgery is commonly used to correct a person's vision. The laser cuts the cornea of the eye, which is peeled back. Then the laser is used to carefully burn away lumps on the lens that make wearing glasses necessary. Without precise surgery, the person being operated on might not only need to keep wearing glasses, but also need eye treatment for damage.

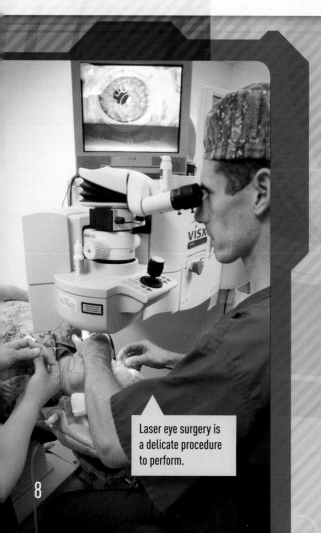

Laser eye surgery is a delicate procedure to perform.

Copycat Robots

Surgeons operating using robot surgical equipment see what they are doing through a high-definition monitor, which feeds in images taken by mini cameras. The surgeons get a bright and clear 3-D view of what they are doing. The robot is a copycat: it copies every movement the surgeon makes with the master controls exactly as the surgeon does it. Surgeons usually sit, resting their arms and hands on pads to make sure they do not get tired. They move their hands and fingers to make the robot move, but on a different scale.

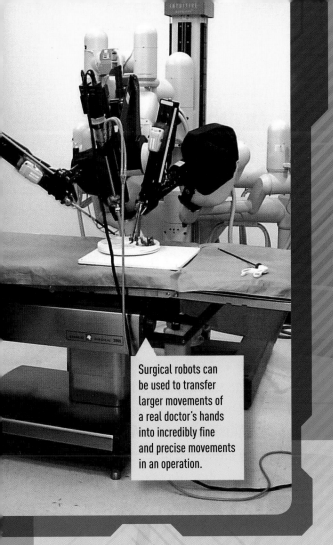

Surgical robots can be used to transfer larger movements of a real doctor's hands into incredibly fine and precise movements in an operation.

Robots Are the Future

Robot surgery in the future could be even more precise because it is likely to be microsurgery. Machines will have even thinner and more maneuverable arms that allow surgeons to reach anywhere through the abdomen using their robots.

Tiny tools will allow surgeons to translate large movements into tiny ones, while built-in motors and specialized joints will stop slight twitches from the surgeon translating into large movements that could cause damage. For example, this will enable surgeons to mend tiny nerves and blood vessels during reconstructive surgery on people with facial or hand damage, so that they will have a full range of feeling afterward. Microsurgery could also allow surgeons to operate directly on damaged parts of the retina to improve sight.

To understand how copycat surgery works, think of how when you zoom in on a photograph on a computer, you can see it is made from tiny squares called pixels. You can move your mouse by normal amounts to move from pixel to pixel, on a microscopic scale. It is the same with robot surgical equipment. A surgeon's hand can move 1 inch (2.5 cm) to move a surgical blade by 0.1 inches (0.25 cm).

CHAPTER 2

Surgeons

Robosurgery has been around for more than 30 years. It started in 1983 in Vancouver, Canada, where surgeons developed Arthrobot to prove that robots could assist with surgery. However, the first actual use of robosurgery was in 1985, when a robot named Puma 560 placed a needle deep in a patient's brain to take a tissue sample. This robot, like several later surgical robots, had a very specific job to do.

In Space and Beyond

By the 1990s, people were starting to see more and more possible uses for robot surgeons. The National Aeronautics and Space Administration (NASA) and the US Army were especially interested in robosurgery. NASA saw the potential of robot surgeons for future settlements in space stations and on other planets. It realized that using robot technology, surgeons on Earth could operate in space.

NASA funded the development of a robotic arm for hand surgery. Its goal was to let the surgeon feel like he or she was operating directly on the patient, for example, by using mechanical joints so the surgeon could feel pushes and pulls, and not indirectly from a console at a distance from the patient. The US Army saw similar potential in robot surgery on the battlefield. Using robosurgery, medics could help save the lives of the wounded without putting themselves at risk. The Army-funded robot surgical system was called AESOP. It was a robotic arm that could be controlled using voice commands.

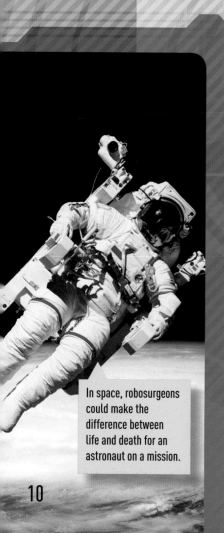

In space, robosurgeons could make the difference between life and death for an astronaut on a mission.

In the future there may be more robosurgeons making the cuts and incisions that are mainly done by human doctors today.

ZEUS and da Vinci

By the late 1990s, there were two working robotic surgical systems. The da Vinci system was based on the NASA developments and ZEUS was based on AESOP. Both systems have been used since then, but da Vinci became the major surgical robot used worldwide today. Da Vinci robots have performed more than 1.5 million surgeries worldwide.

Robots Are the Future

NASA is developing the next robosurgeon. It will be used on astronauts in space who need surgery. NASA has worked with the Virtual Incision Corporation (VIC) to develop a fist-sized robot that can be slid into a patient's body through an incision in the navel (belly button). In the abdomen, the robot moves to find and operate on problems, such as an inflamed appendix or stomach ulcer.

Da Vinci

Da Vinci is an impressive surgical robot. It is made up of two separate parts that are connected by an electrical cable. The first part is the tower, which is made up of four robotic arms mounted on a wheeled base. The second component is the console where the surgeon sits.

The Tower

The tower is placed over the patient during surgery. Three of the arms do the surgery through tiny incisions in the patient. They can move in any direction, much like a human arm, but with the improvement of a multi-jointed wrist. Each arm can hold an array of different tools.

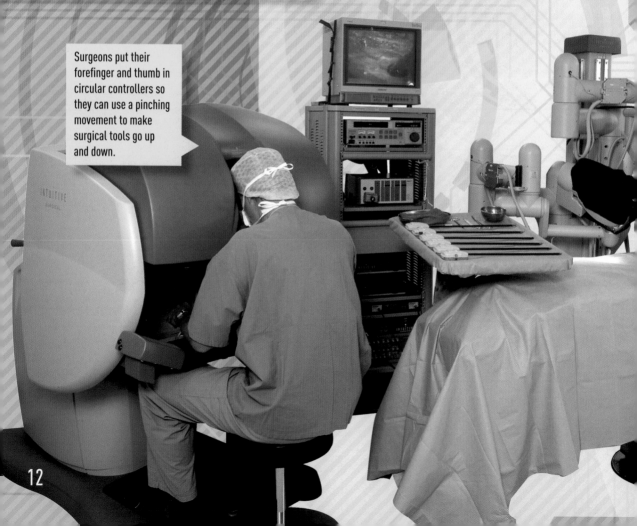

Surgeons put their forefinger and thumb in circular controllers so they can use a pinching movement to make surgical tools go up and down.

The fourth arm holds da Vinci's two endoscopes. Together they produce a high-definition, well-lit 3-D image of the site that needs surgery. The endoscopes are heated to make sure that the lens never fogs up in the moist insides of the patient and so that they send clear images.

The Console

At the console, the surgeon looks into a screen that shows a magnified view of what the cameras are seeing. The surgeon moves sensitive controllers that send signals to a computer, which tell the three surgical arms how to move. Every movement the surgeon makes is mimicked by the robotic arms, down to the slightest fingertip movement. A 2-D video feed of what the surgeon sees is shown on a monitor so that the rest of the surgical team, including nurses in the operating theater, can see what is going on.

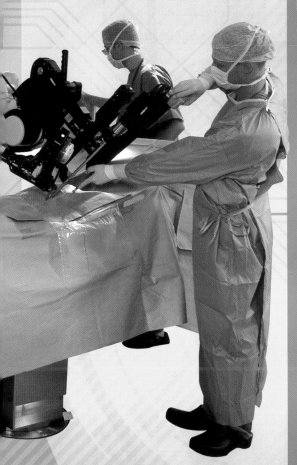

Robots Are the Future

Da Vinci does not work unless a surgeon controls its movements, but in the future there will be more autonomous robosurgeon devices that move and work unassisted. The first autonomous operation was performed in 2006, when a surgeon in the United States operated on a patient with heart problems 4,000 miles (6,437 km) away. The robot's movements through a blood vessel into the heart were controlled by a magnetic navigation system. Since then, there have been other long-distance surgeries. In the future, the dreams of space and battlefield operations may become reality.

Applications

Da Vinci is an adaptable system because the pencil-width tips of its arms can be mounted with a wide range of tools for different surgeries. These include not only scissors and scalpels, but also:

- An electrical tool that heats up and burns at the push of a button. It can be used to seal off bleeding blood vessels.
- Clamps to temporarily close off vessels.
- Tools to grip and move tissue out of the way.
- Needle grippers to hold needles for stitching up incisions.

Da Vinci's Uses

There are many surgical applications for da Vinci. It is used in heart surgery, for example, to repair heart valves so that hearts keep beating. It is also used to remove sections of the intestine so that it can continue to function. In the United States, da Vinci carries out four out of every five operations to remove tumors from prostate glands in men, and around one-third of operations to remove uteruses in women. These complicated operations on delicate areas require less cutting and leave less scarring and post-operative pain when performed by robots, compared with surgeries by surgeons.

These are just some of the surgical instruments used by da Vinci.

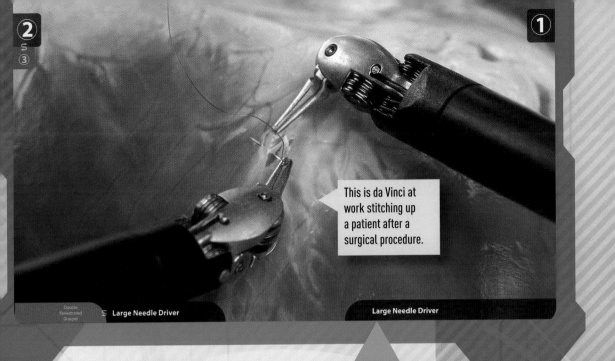

This is da Vinci at work stitching up a patient after a surgical procedure.

Double Fewstrated Grasper

S Large Needle Driver

Large Needle Driver

Robots Are the Future

The Costs Involved

Da Vinci and other robot surgical systems are very expensive to buy, at around $1 million each. The surgeons who operate them may need lengthy and expensive training, too. However, the robots are bringing rewards for hospitals. Patients operated on by robots stay in the hospital for less time and have fewer surgical complications. They then recover faster, and need fewer pain medications and less intensive care, so their hospital stay costs less.

Da Vinci may help surgeons in their work even more in the future. Surgical locations, such as tumors, will be injected with fluorescent dyes that show up only in infrared or ultraviolet (UV) light. The da Vinci video feed then views the operation site using that light and it makes the tumor glow, in the same way that soldiers use infrared goggles to spot enemies in the dark. The imaging device may also be able to use similar technology to make tissue show up in red if surgeons get too near to it and risk damaging healthy tissue.

15

Chapter 3

Bot Images

When doctors need to find out what is wrong with someone's internal organs or they need to do a difficult operation, robotic imaging can be a huge help. Using robotic machines to take images of a patient's insides makes medical procedures safer and easier for the patients involved.

X-Rays

Early images of human insides were taken using x-rays, which were discovered in 1895. X-rays are invisible energy waves, rather like light, which can travel through softer materials like skin but not harder materials, so they can be used to take photographs of bones and teeth.

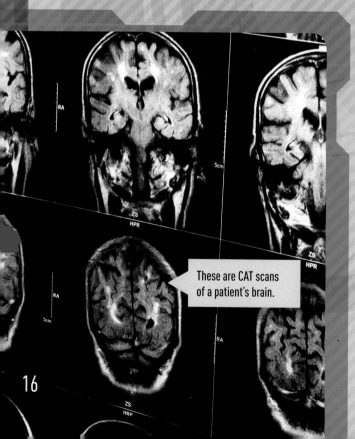

These are CAT scans of a patient's brain.

CAT Scanners

Modern robotic imaging is sophisticated. CAT is short for Computed Axial Tomography, and a CAT scan machine (sometimes called a CT scanner) takes hundreds of x-ray pictures of the inside of a patient's body. The patient lies very still inside a CAT scan machine, and then the table on which they are lying goes in and out of the machine at least twice. The robotic imager scans through the part of the body that the doctor is concerned about, such as the head or chest, taking many pictures at different angles, slice by slice. Patients do not feel anything as the CAT scan is taken, but may hear whirring and buzzing as the machine works. The machine then puts together these numerous flat 2-D x-ray images to create a 3-D picture, which doctors can use to examine the patient's insides from many angles. CAT scans can show infections, swelling, injury, or disease without the doctor having to cut open and look inside the patient's body.

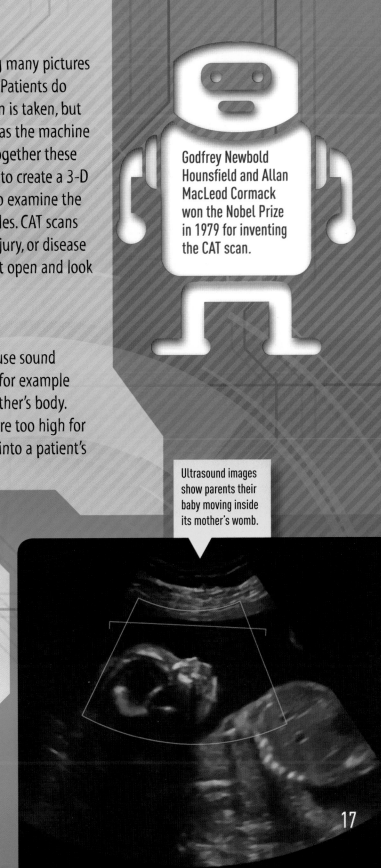

Godfrey Newbold Hounsfield and Allan MacLeod Cormack won the Nobel Prize in 1979 for inventing the CAT scan.

Ultrasound

Ultrasound scanning machines use sound waves to make moving images, for example of an unborn baby inside its mother's body. High-frequency sounds, which are too high for the human ear to hear, are sent into a patient's body through a small handheld camera called a probe. As the probe moves over the patient's body, ultrasound waves reflect off the soft organs inside the body and bounce back as echoes. The echoes are displayed as moving images on a screen and these give the doctor information about the size, shape, and texture of the body part being scanned.

Ultrasound images show parents their baby moving inside its mother's womb.

MRI Scanners

MRI stands for Magnetic Resonance Imaging. A robotic MRI imager uses a combination of radio waves and a strong magnet to produce detailed pictures of the inside of the body. MRI scans provide much more detailed pictures of a patient's body than ordinary x-ray images, allowing doctors to clearly see details of soft tissue, bone, joints, and ligaments. This makes MRI scans particularly useful for identifying problems in the spine, brain, and the joints. MRI scanners are also helpful for looking at other parts of the body, often when other types of scans have not given doctors a full enough picture to make a diagnosis.

In the Scanner

An MRI scanner consists of a scanner, which is usually shaped like a large rectangle with a hole in the center (much like the center of a donut), a patient table, and a computer workstation. Before an MRI scan, a patient has to take off any objects containing metal, such as eyeglasses, jewelry, and belts. Then, the patient lies on the motorized and computer-controlled table, and the table moves the patient into the scanner's center hole. In the hole, the patient is surrounded by a magnetic field and scanned with radio waves, which are absorbed by the body.

Medical staff can view the results of the MRI scan on computer screens in a room next door to the scanner.

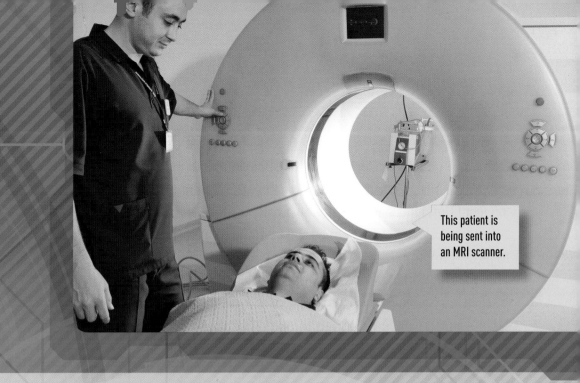

This patient is being sent into an MRI scanner.

The MRI scanner is operated from a room next door with a window, so the operator can see what is going on. There is also an intercom system, so the operator can speak to the patient to tell them what to do and what is happening. When the scanning is complete, the robotic imaging scanner then analyzes these waves to create the MRI images. MRI robotic imagers can be used to do tasks such as producing images that show different parts of a patient's brain.

Making Patients Comfortable

When patients lie on the table and slide into the closed, narrow tunnel of an MRI scanner, this can make them feel a little uncomfortable and nervous. To help with this, some medical centers have open MRI scanners with larger openings, or they use shorter openings that allow the patient's head to remain outside the machine.

MRI scanners are used to show doctors tiny changes that happen during the course of an illness.

One way for doctors to look at the small intestine is to insert an endoscope. This is a flexible tube and camera system more than 3.5 feet (1 m) long. It is put through a patient's mouth and down their throat. The patient has to be sedated, and it takes some time to recover from this procedure. All this changed with the invention of PillCam. PillCam is a miniature robot that would not be out of place in a sci-fi movie! After a patient swallows one of these tiny, tablet-shaped wonders, it travels through their digestive system, checking for problems without the patient feeling a thing.

Enter the PillCam

PillCam is a tiny, battery-powered capsule that contains a video camera, a light source, batteries, and a radio. It is only 0.4 inches (1 cm) in diameter, 1 inch (2.5 cm) long, weighs fewer than 0.14 ounces (4 g), and is shaped like a tablet you might buy over the counter at a pharmacy. After a patient swallows it, PillCam takes about 50,000 high-speed photographs as it works its way through the digestive system over the course of an eight-hour period—about two images per second! It transmits the images to a recorder attached to a belt worn around the patient's waist, which then downloads them onto a computer. A doctor can then view the video images and look for things like small growths, to help make a diagnosis about cancer and other digestive problems. The capsule is disposable and after about 24 hours it passes out of the body naturally and can be flushed away.

Pillcam is a robot that is small enough for a person to swallow.

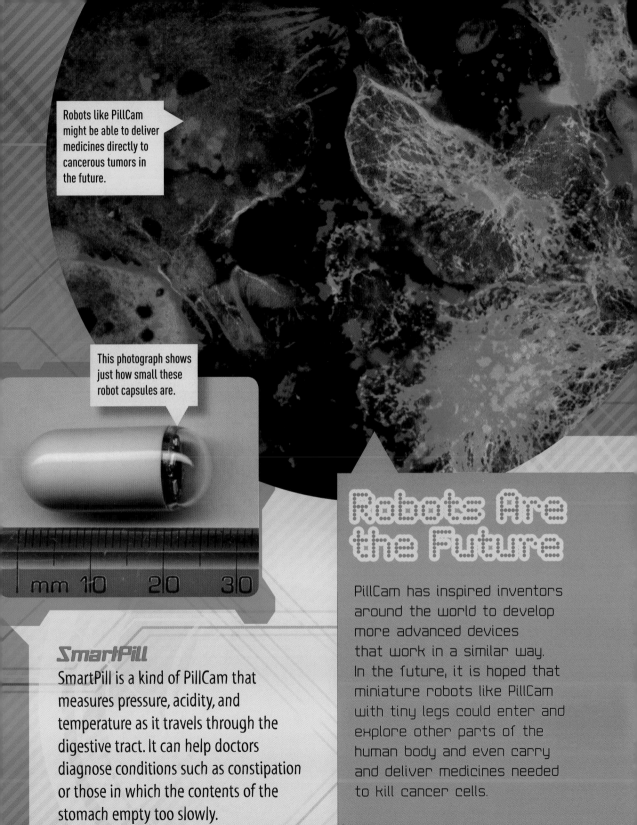

Robots like PillCam might be able to deliver medicines directly to cancerous tumors in the future.

This photograph shows just how small these robot capsules are.

mm 10 20 30

SmartPill

SmartPill is a kind of PillCam that measures pressure, acidity, and temperature as it travels through the digestive tract. It can help doctors diagnose conditions such as constipation or those in which the contents of the stomach empty too slowly.

Robots Are the Future

PillCam has inspired inventors around the world to develop more advanced devices that work in a similar way. In the future, it is hoped that miniature robots like PillCam with tiny legs could enter and explore other parts of the human body and even carry and deliver medicines needed to kill cancer cells.

Chapter 4

Robot Pharmacists

A major part of health care is the use of drugs to prevent and treat illnesses and to relieve symptoms of both serious diseases and minor health complaints. For example, around 80 percent of older adults live with one or more chronic conditions, which unless treated, could cause serious harm or even death. These include high blood pressure, diabetes, arthritis, and cancer. In the United States alone, doctors write around 4 billion prescriptions for chronic conditions. Medical drugs, along with lifestyle changes, such as increased exercise or improved diet, are essential for managing these conditions.

Robotic machines are increasingly used to analyze blood and other samples.

The Pharmacist's Role

Pharmacists are medical professionals with expert knowledge of drugs and how they work in the human body. They undergo many years of education and training, and most work in the community, for example, in drugstores and in hospitals. Prescribing the right medicines can be a matter of life or death for patients, but unfortunately mistakes are sometimes made. Studies suggest that in the United States, around 1.5 million people are harmed each year by preventable pharmacist errors.

Some of these mistakes are caused by drug interactions, when a drug taken to help one condition prevents another from working. Others are caused by prescribing the wrong dose or the wrong drug.

Robot Researchers

Pharmacists increasingly rely on robots in different ways. In medical laboratories, pharmacists use robots to help develop and test new drugs, spot fake drugs, and analyze patients' blood and tissue samples. One part of this work is to calculate the effect of different doses of drugs on tissue samples to find out how safe they are. This involves examining a large number of samples, collecting data, comparing it to databases of results, and keeping large and complicated records. Robots can do this faster, cheaper, and accurately.

Robots fill a gap because there are not enough people who want to do such routine and time-consuming laboratory work. For example, robot systems can analyze more than 1,500 small samples of different doses of a drug in around half a minute.

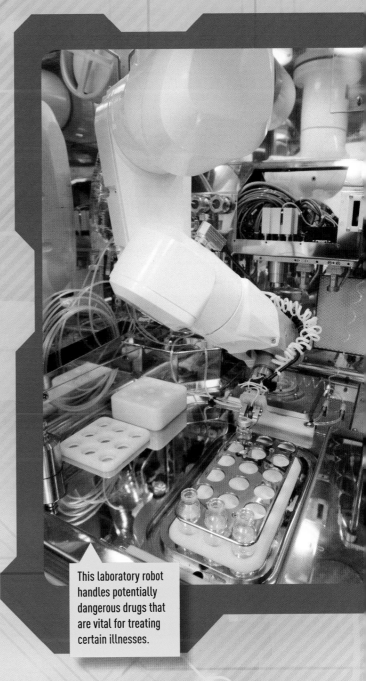

This laboratory robot handles potentially dangerous drugs that are vital for treating certain illnesses.

Robot Drugstore

In large hospitals and in warehouses supplying online pharmacies, there are large numbers of prescriptions coming in all the time. Unlike in a small drugstore, the team of pharmacists may struggle to keep up with dispensing drugs for the prescriptions in time to meet demand. When rushed, pharmacists are more likely to make mistakes.

ROBOT-Rx

Mistakes can be fatal, which is why more and more pharmacies are investing in robot drugstores. One of the most popular in hospitals is called the ROBOT-Rx® system. This is a sealed room with thousands of drugs loaded onto racks in packets. A robotic arm can locate specific drugs, pick them from the racks, and put them into a small box. The box is then emptied and sealed into an envelope, which emerges from the room on a conveyor belt. Medical staff take batches of envelopes to where they are needed in the hospital.

How Does ROBOT-Rx Work?

ROBOT-Rx relies on bar codes to work. Bar codes are unique identifying sequences of lines of different thicknesses, like those you see on the side of supermarket products. Each drug type has a specific bar code. Each prescription, which also has a unique bar code linked to individual patient records, is converted into a request for particular drug bar codes by a built-in computer system.

Then a bar code scanner on the picker finds the right drugs to complete the prescription. The stock levels of drugs on ROBOT-Rx's computer system are changed each time a drug or medicine is dispensed, so the system alerts staff when it is time to restock drugs. Drugs also have date-of-manufacture information built into their bar codes, so ROBOT-Rx can also make sure that drugs are used within safe time limits.

ROBOT-Rx Benefits

Robot pharmacies achieve nearly perfect prescription filling accuracy. They cut the amount of time that pharmacists would normally spend on checking prescriptions by 90 percent. The great advantage of this is that pharmacists and technicians are free from the repetitive tasks of finding, picking, and packing drugs for dispensing. This means they can spend time on more productive activities, such as dealing with specific patient drug needs and finding out about new drug therapies.

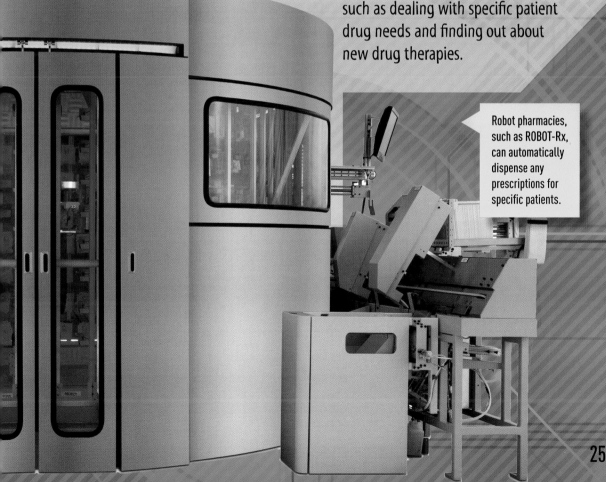

Robot pharmacies, such as ROBOT-Rx, can automatically dispense any prescriptions for specific patients.

IV Robots

Many drugs are given to patients as intravenous (IV) liquids through needles into their blood system, either from syringes or from bags. Preparing IV drugs can be problematic for people. It is complicated to make the right mixes of some drugs, especially if adult-strength doses have to be mixed for use in sick children. Hospitals waste money if IV liquids are thrown away when they have been wrongly prepared. Every time a preparation is mixed, there is a risk of contamination by other drugs or by bacteria in the air. Some very strong IV drugs used in chemotherapy to treat cancers can harm patients taking the wrong doses or technicians handling the drugs.

RIVA robots store and prepare drugs in an enclosed room.

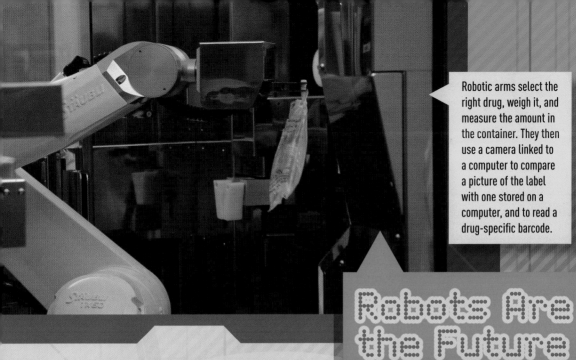

Robotic arms select the right drug, weigh it, and measure the amount in the container. They then use a camera linked to a computer to compare a picture of the label with one stored on a computer, and to read a drug-specific barcode.

Robots Are the Future

Robots Get It Right!

More and more hospitals are turning to robots to prepare their IV drugs. Robot IV systems automatically calculate exactly the right mixes, at high speed, and in completely sterile conditions. RIVA is a robotic system that has stores of drugs and a robotic arm. It operates in an enclosed room and can work for 5 hours at a time, preparing up to 60 IV doses an hour. The system uses syringes to measure doses and prepares sealed syringes and bags of mixed IV solutions, identified by bar codes on labels. The sealed drugs leave RIVA on a conveyer belt. RIVA uses machines that make pulses of UV light to kill any bacteria in the system and to sterilize needles, syringes, and bags.

Scientists at Google in the United States are developing robots that can be injected into blood. The robots will be able to diagnose health problems when they first appear. These tiny robots will be one-hundredth of the size of a red blood cell, and will latch onto specific sites around the body.

They will then monitor changes in chemicals around them. These changes are signs of the start of diseases. They will send the information to devices, such as Google watches, that will alert people if something is wrong. This system could help physicians cure or treat problems before they develop into more serious conditions.

Chapter 5

Robot Staff

Imagine a hospital where some of the staff moving up and down the corridors and attending to chores are robots. In fact, this is already happening in some parts of the world, since hospitals are fairly robot-friendly places. Medical buildings usually have flat, well-lit halls and floors, elevators that robots can roll into to travel between floors, and few obstacles because walkways are kept clear for stretchers and carts. To help robots move around in a hospital and avoid moving obstacles like stretchers and carts, robot staff have sensors that tell them when something is in their way.

Robot Cleaners

Robots are ideal for the dull and dirty jobs in a hospital, like cleaning. Not only does the robot cleaner do the job more quickly, but it is also more effective than when a human cleans a room with the strongest type of disinfectant or bleach. Before the robot cleaner rolls into a room on its wheels, everyone, including the patients, has to leave it. Then, the robot blasts UV light that is 25,000 times more powerful than sunlight, over all surfaces, including under the bed, between folds on curtains, and on surfaces that are hard to reach, such as keyboards and complicated medical equipment. After about 10 to 15 minutes, the bacteria or viruses that may have been living on the surfaces of the room will be killed.

An End to Superbugs?

The robot does not scrub surfaces or remove dirt—these are still jobs for humans! Instead, robot cleaners kill microscopic germs, including the ones known as "superbugs," which patients can catch

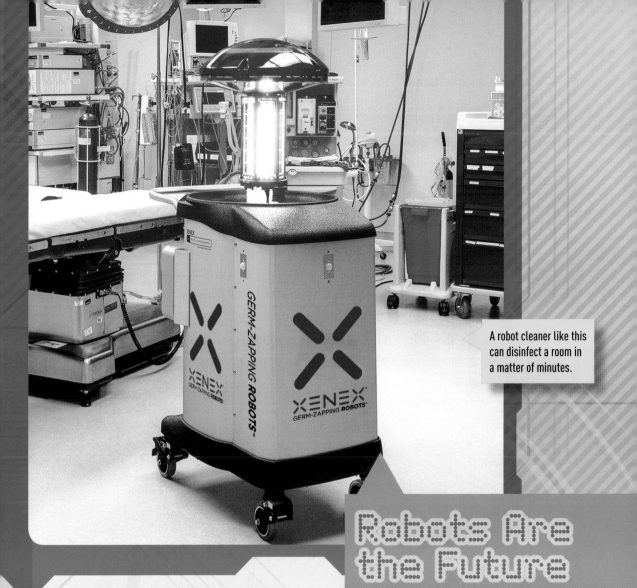

A robot cleaner like this can disinfect a room in a matter of minutes.

Robots Are the Future

while they are at the hospital, often for treatment for another condition. These superbug infections can be devastating and even deadly, and affect around 1 out of every 20 patients. In the United States, more people are believed to die from a lack of hospital infection control than from AIDS, breast cancer, and car accidents combined.

Robot cleaners are only in use in a few hospitals around the world, but in the future they could become an important weapon in the fight against major diseases such as Ebola. Robot cleaners can destroy at least 95 percent of all germs in a room, so they are ideal for preventing the spread of infections.

Telemedics

Would you mind if your doctor spoke to you through a screen on top of a robot? A new type of robot, sometimes known as a telemedic, is helping doctors speak to and examine patients far away. Telemedics are proving incredibly useful and can save lives, for example, when a medical specialist can see and question a patient in a rural area where there is a shortage of doctors. Telemedics can also examine a patient in an emergency, when a speedy diagnosis and the right medical advice can make the difference between life and death.

No matter where a patient is, doctors can be beamed to their bedside in minutes thanks to telemedics.

Doctors and Telemedics

Telemedics move around on wheels and are about 5 feet (1.5 m) tall. The robot has an auto-drive function that allows it to navigate its way to and from different patients' rooms, using sensors to avoid bumping into obstacles or people. When a doctor is needed, they can log into a telemedic from wherever they are by using a computer, laptop, or tablet computer. At the top of the robot, there is a large screen that projects a live video of the doctor's face.

Log in to Save Lives

Once the telemedic is inside the hospital room, doctors and patients can see, hear, and speak to each other via the cameras, microphones, and speakers that the robot carries. Of course, the doctor cannot touch the patient, but there will always be a nurse or other type of medical assistant with the patient who can do things like take temperatures or other readings that the doctor might need to help with a diagnosis. The robot can also give the doctor access to computer records of medical images or the results of tests that the patient may have had taken.

Robots Are the Future

In the future, telemedics may be given arms. This is not so they can touch things, but to make the robots more expressive, so they can gesticulate with their arms and hands to appear more human to patients in distress. The doctor's arm movements could be sensed using a motion-capture device, and then relayed to the robot.

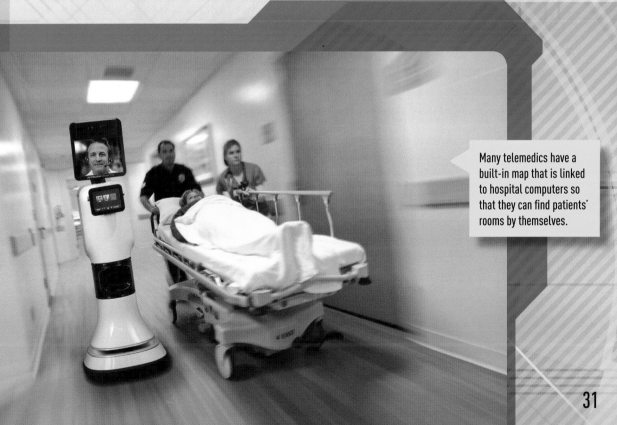

Many telemedics have a built-in map that is linked to hospital computers so that they can find patients' rooms by themselves.

Robots on the Wards

Hospitals are busy places, and doctors and nurses have to deal with many patients a day. They do important work, but this medical work is constantly interrupted by the need to do time-consuming but mundane tasks like walking down to a pharmacy to fetch medicines. That is where robots can step in!

HOSPI Robot

The HOSPI robot is an autonomous robot designed to deliver samples, drugs, and devices around hospitals so that laboratory technicians and nurses do not have to do this job. This frees up human hospital staff to use the time to do more important work. The HOSPI robot has a map of the hospital programmed into it in advance. It uses this map to plan its route and it navigates using just its 27 ultrasonic sensors, which help it maneuver around people and objects. The HOSPI robot has a locked cabinet to make sure that no one but staff with the correct code can get at the drugs it is carrying. This ensures it delivers the drugs safely and accurately.

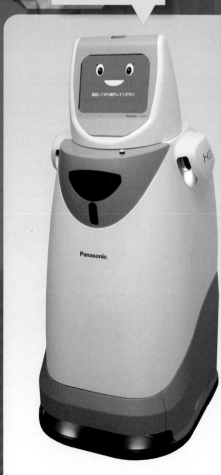

HOSPI robot carries out simple tasks to free up the time of hospital doctors and nurses.

Tug can haul up to 500 pounds (227 kg) of goods at a time.

The Tug robot has infrared light "whiskers" that detect obstacles in its path. The robot stops about 18 inches (46 cm) away from the obstacle and either waits until it moves, or goes around it.

Tug Bot

Tug is a service robot designed to haul goods such as bed linens and medicines. Different carts can be attached to the robot's body, depending on what goods it needs to carry. Sonar, infrared, and laser rangefinders help it find its way around obstacles. Tug's sensors help it track its location within a programmed map of a building. The robot's computer contains a map of the hospital and a wireless communication system that relays information about where the robot is. It uses wireless signals to select a floor on an elevator and open and close doors by itself. It runs on batteries and can work for ten hours before it needs a break to be recharged. It can voice messages such as, "Your deliveries are here," and it uses warning tones and lights to let people know when it is starting, stopping, and reversing.

Chapter 6

Mobility

Robotics can also be used to help people with mobility issues—people who have difficulty moving around independently. This is sometimes called rehabilitation robotics. The goal of rehabilitation robotics is to use robotics to help paraplegic or disabled people, as well as those who cannot move or who have difficulty moving arms or legs or supporting themselves. Using arms to move a normal wheelchair can cause a strain on shoulder muscles and wrist and elbow joints, but powered scooters, wheelchairs, or other devices can make a huge difference to people's lives. They can give people a newfound independence and the freedom to go wherever they want.

Powerchairs

People with limited mobility and those who tire easily when walking use mobility scooters. Ordinary mobility scooters have three or four wheels and are steered using a bicycle-style handlebar. Powerchairs usually look more like traditional wheelchairs, with some models having batteries and a motor attached to each wheel. The powerchair is usually driven using one hand on a joystick controller on the arm of the powerchair. Powerchair users tend to spend more time in their chairs than scooter users spend on their scooters. As a result of this, powerchairs are usually more adaptable than disabled scooters, and some models can have specialized seats and controllers attached to suit the requirements of the user. For example, the powerchair can be controlled by hand, by a chin controller, or using a sip-and-puff pipe operated with the mouth.

The footrests can be specific to the user's needs and can include swing-away or articulating footrests. Powerchairs are also more likely to be used inside, although some are equally capable indoors and outdoors.

Powerchairs like this one can transform life for their users.

Adapting Powerchairs

Some people may not be able to support themselves at all. Their powerchair can provide support for their head and limbs, and be used to do many other things. For example, some powerchairs have a small portable computer attached that can be controlled using a simple head or eye movement. This allows people to control not only the movement of the powerchair, but also to control electronic devices in a home, such as the television, via a programmable infrared controller attached to the computer system. They will also be able to operate doors and lights using a remote-control device.

Tek Robotic Mobilization Device

The Tek Robotic Mobilization Device (RMD) is a mobility aid that supports people in the standing position. This helps people who use or need a wheelchair in different ways. For one thing, it is important for paraplegic people to be in a standing position for at least an hour every day, because this kind of exercise helps keep their body healthy. RMD also enables paraplegic people to move through narrow passages, get in and out of ordinary chairs without assistance, and do many of the other things independently that they could not before they could use the RMD.

Standing Up

The real innovation of the Tek RMD is that it makes it easy and quick to stand up and sit down. It is hard to get in and out of a wheelchair without help because paraplegic people have to launch themselves from a sitting position. The Tek RMD is different. It works in a similar way to office chairs that can be raised or lowered with the pull of a handle. It has a special suspension system that balances users' weight with a spring, so that they can get into a standing position on their own using just a gentle pull. The fact that it is easy to use encourages people to get into a standing position more often and allows them to do things that are easier to do in a standing position, too.

Tek RMD can run for two days or more before it needs recharging.

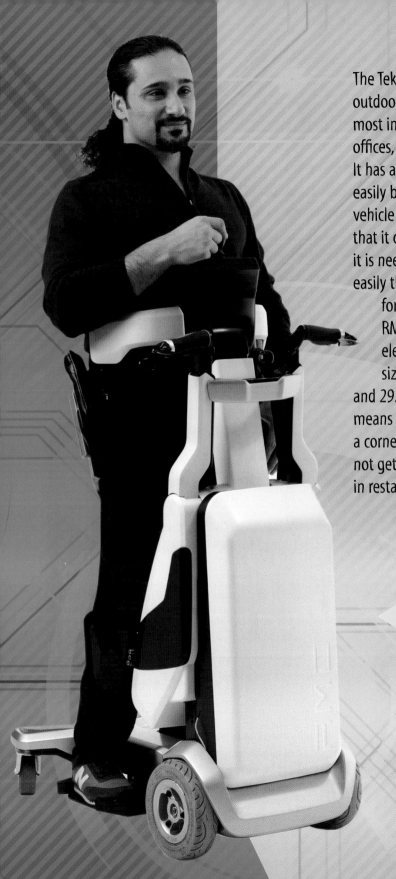

The Tek RMD is not designed for outdoor use, but it can be used in most indoor spaces like homes, offices, colleges, and shopping malls. It has a remote control so that it can easily be loaded into and out of a vehicle that has a ramp. This means that it can be transported to where it is needed. It is narrow so it fits easily through spaces too narrow for wheelchairs to go. The Tek RMD is battery-operated, like an electric wheelchair. Tek's small size—16.5 inches (42 cm) wide and 29.5 inches (75 cm) long—means it can be tucked away in a corner when not in use, so it does not get in the way, for example, in restaurants.

The Tek RMD gives paraplegic people more freedom because it allows them to spend more time in places not specifically designed for those in wheelchairs.

Exosuits

When people have accidents and suffer spinal cord injuries, they may suddenly be unable to walk. This is a life-changing and incredibly challenging situation. Now scientists have come up with a new robotic device to help those with spinal cord injuries to walk again: exosuits. These are robotic exoskeletons that people wear over their clothes and attached to their limbs in some way. The exoskeleton powers hip and knee motion to enable individuals with spinal cord injuries to stand up and walk.

ReWalk

ReWalk is a robotic exosuit that uses powered leg attachments to enable paraplegic people to stand upright, walk, and even to climb stairs. This exosuit is powered by a battery stored in a backpack where the computer is also housed. The suit consists of a brace that supports the wearer's body and sensors. By a shift in the wearer's balance, the sensors recognize a change in position, and make knee or hip movements happen to enable the wearer to take a step forward.

ReWalk helps people walk with the same kind of movement that a healthy pedestrian uses.

HAL responds to thoughts such as "I want to stand up!" or "I want to walk!"

HAL

HAL, which is short for Hybrid Assistive Limb, is an exoskeleton robotics suit. It is not widely used yet but when it is, it will be able to help a physically challenged person to move in a brand-new way. The suit includes small motors and a tiny wireless computer in a pouch attached to the belt. When someone wants to move, their brain sends signals through nerves to the muscles to make it happen. When this happens, very faint signals also leak on to the surface of the skin. When someone wears HAL, detectors are attached to the wearer's skin and use information from the brain's signals to help HAL understand what sort of movement the wearer wants to make. The motors in the suit then help the wearer to make those movements.

Robots Are the Future

The amazing thing about HAL is that in the future it may also help people with spinal cord injuries walk and move independently again. When the body responds to signals sent from the brain, the feeling of being able to walk is relayed back to the brain. Gradually, the brain learns the way to send signals that will make the HAL wearer actually walk without the suit.

Chapter 7

Bionic Parts

In the 1970s, there was a television program in which a man, who suffered a near-fatal car crash, was rebuilt as the "Bionic Man." He had more powerful vision, could run faster, and was stronger than any regular person because he had been implanted with replacements for biological parts. He was part robot. Back then the idea of a bionic man was pure fiction, but today, there are people whose lives have been greatly improved by having bionic parts. Bionic parts mimic a natural function using electronics and engineering.

In this x-ray of a human chest, the white glowing object is a surgically implanted pacemaker.

Artificial Parts

Many artificial parts have been put into people to help them live more normally. For example, in 1960, the first people were fitted with pacemakers under their skin. Pacemakers are electrical devices that create regular electrical pulses that stimulate the human heart to beat. This has changed the lives of people whose heartbeat was irregular. Today there are completely artificial electronically controlled hearts, for example, made by SynCardia, which can be surgically implanted into patients while they wait for a heart transplant.

Prosthetic Limbs

There is a long history of replacement or prosthetic legs or parts of legs to aid mobility. These range from surgical hip replacement joints to prosthetic legs. However, most of these, whether they are wooden legs or high-tech carbon fiber blades, are not like robots because they cannot move automatically. Some of these have knee joints allowing the part below the knee to swing forward, then lock to keep the leg straight while the other leg swings forward during the walking motion.

Some prosthetic legs have bionic or "smart" knees. Smart knees such as Ossur Rheo or the Bock C-leg have built-in sensors to monitor the forces and movements in the knee that adjust to a particular person. This depends on the person's weight and way of walking. The Rheo knee joint can become stiffer when running and less stiff when walking slowly because the liquid inside can get stickier or thinner. It does this using magnets that get stronger or weaker, depending on how fast the two parts of the leg move.

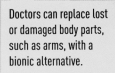

The batteries in the Rheo knee joint can last up to three days before they need to be charged.

Doctors can replace lost or damaged body parts, such as arms, with a bionic alternative.

Bionic Hands

Smart knees can mimic the natural walking or running behavior of a leg, but an arm is more complicated. Arms have a wider range of joints and are capable of everything from lifting loads to gentle touch. Even today, some prosthetic arms are tipped with hooks or very basic false fingers for lifting and are incapable of gripping many small items or performing delicate movements. However, that is all changing with the development of bionic hands. As with other limb prosthetics, the development of bionic hands is being funded partly by the military, because many soldiers in a lot of conflicts worldwide have lost limbs during their active duty.

Bionic hands allow injured people to get back to normal life as soon as possible.

> Bionic hands are being developed that even have a sense of touch to help people feel things with their fingers again!

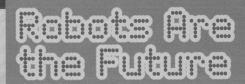

Myoelectric Hands

Bionic hands such as BeBionic and iLIMB are myoelectric. This means they move based on signals from muscles in the remaining part of the arm. When you think of picking up a coin, your brain sends messages that travel through the muscles via nerve fibers. The bionic hands work because sensors can intercept these messages.

BeBionic is a carbon fiber hand with individual motors in each finger, allowing movement and grip. The fingers can produce 14 different grips, including open palm grip (used to take the lid off a jar) and key grip between the thumb and side of the forefinger. The hand can vary its strength and speed of movement so it can pick up an egg without breaking it or crush a metal can. Some people wear the hand covered with a life-like plastic skin, complete with skin folds and nails.

Robots Are the Future

The most advanced myoelectric hands allow a range of movements, but bionic hands generally do not let users feel through their fingers. All the electrical messages move from the body to the hand and not the other way. A prototype hand from 2013 allowed the user to feel whether things were soft or hard, round or square. Inside each finger is an artificial tendon that creates an electrical signal based on what it feels, which is then transmitted by wires surgically embedded in nerves in the arm.

Artificial Senses

Touch is just one of the senses that has been recreated using bionics. People with hearing loss that is so bad that hearing aids do not help may be given cochlear implants. These bionic hearing devices include a microphone behind the ear to detect sounds, and a transmitter under the skin to convert the sounds into electrical signals. The implant sends the signals to an electrode on the inner ear that passes the signals on to nerves. The nerves carry messages to the brain, which interprets them as sounds.

Tiny implants give people with sight problems a new bionic eye!

Seeing Is Believing

Some people who are blind can now see using artificial retinas. The retina is the light-sensitive layer at the back of the eye. People with retinas that do not work properly have operations to put an implant on their retina. They wear glasses with built-in cameras to detect the patterns of light and dark that make up images. The glasses transmit information about the image to the implant. Electrodes on the implant pass signals that represent the image onto a nerve. This transmits signals to the brain, which interprets the light pattern as something we see.

Smelling and Tasting

In the future, bionic parts may re-create the senses of smelling and tasting. Bionic retinas and ears may be developed that are sensitive enough to let people see or hear normally. By then there may be nanorobot surgeons that can operate on damaged parts of eyes and ears. This—and all other parts of medicine and health care—will be increasingly reliant on robots.

Glasses with built-in cameras help people with bionic eye implants to see.

Robots Are the Future

In 2011, a woman who was paralyzed and could not move her arms or legs poured water into her own mouth to drink. She did this by using her mind to control a robotic arm. This was made possible by doctors who implanted a tiny sensor on her brain. They asked the woman to think of lifting the bottle and recorded the patterns of electrical signals produced by the brain. Using a computer they converted this pattern into instructions to move the robotic arm. In the future it may be possible to control the movement of all bionic parts directly, just by thinking about them.

Glossary

autonomous acting on its own, without outside control

bacteria microscopic living things, some of which help us and some of which cause disease

bionic robotic

blood transfusions processes of taking blood from one person and giving it to someone else

chronic continuing for a very long time

contamination when something is spoiled or damaged by something else being added to it

diagnosis the act of identifying a disease or illness

digestive system the parts of the body that digest, or break down, the food that is eaten

dispense to give out

dose a specified amount

electrode a part that passes electricity in and out of it

endoscope a device with a light that is used to look inside a body cavity or organ

exoskeleton a rigid external covering for the body

fluorescent very bright

general anesthetic a drug given to a patient to send them into a coma so that a surgeon can operate on them

gesticulate to make gestures with the hands

high frequency the high repetition of sound or radio waves in a set time

humanoid like a human

implants parts placed into a body during surgery

incisions cuts made into the body

infection a disease caused by bacteria and other germs entering the body

infrared rays of light that cannot be seen

injections needles filled with medicine that are pushed into the body

intravenous in a vein

joints places where two things or parts, such as bones, are joined

laser a very narrow beam of highly concentrated light

ligaments tough pieces of tissue that hold bones together or keep organs in place

magnetic field an area where the magnetic force of an object can be felt

motors machines that make things move

myoelectric a system that helps people move based on signals from muscles in the remaining part of a limb

navigation finding the way

organs body parts, such as the heart and brain

paraplegic a person who is unable to move or use their legs

pharmacists people who prepare and sell prescribed medicines

prescribing telling someone which medicine to use and in what dose to use it

prescriptions notes from a doctor describing the medicine and dosage a person should take

prosthetic describes an artificial device that replaces a missing or injured part of the body

radiographs images made using x-rays or similar

radio waves invisible waves used for sending signals through the air

rangefinders devices used to judge distance

reconstructive building something again that was damaged

remote control operating a machine from a distance

retinas parts at the back of the eye that receive images and send signals to the brain about what is seen

sensors devices that sense things such as heat or movement

spinal cord the main pathway for information connecting the brain and nerves

sterile free from bacteria and other germs

sterilize to make something free from bacteria and other germs

suspension system the parts of a moving object that help it absorb the shock of bumps as it moves across ground

tendon the part of the body that connects a muscle to a bone

ultraviolet (UV) a type of light energy that we cannot see

viruses extremely small living things that cause disease

x-rays invisible rays of light that can pass through objects to see inside them

For More Information

Books

Furstinger, Nancy. *Helper Robots* (Lightning Bolt Books). Minneapolis, MN: Lerner Publications, 2014.

Leider, Rick Allen. *Robots: Explore the World of Robots and How They Work for Us* (The Fact Atlas Series). New York, NY: Sky Pony Press, 2015.

Shulman, Mark. *TIME For Kids Explorers: Robots*. New York, NY: Time For Kids, 2014.

Websites

Explore the world of robots with legs at:
www.ai.mit.edu/projects/leglab

Learn more about robots at:
www.brainpop.com/technology/ computerscience/robots/preview.weml

Find out about the history of robotics at:
www.sciencekids.co.nz/sciencefacts/ technology/historyofrobotics.html

Publisher's note to educators and parents: Our editors have carefully reviewed these websites to ensure that they are suitable for students. Many websites change frequently, however, and we cannot guarantee that a site's future contents will continue to meet our high standards of quality and educational value. Be advised that students should be closely supervised whenever they access the Internet.

Index